I0820291

Clap, Stomp, and Sing

Black Rabbit Books
P.O. Box 227
Mankato, MN 56001
www.blackrabbitbooks.com

Library edition published in 2026 by Black Rabbit Books.
This library-bound edition is reprinted by arrangement with Rebel Girls, Inc.

Text by Calliope Glass | Illustrations by Laura Borio
Art direction by Giulia Flamini | Cover design by Kristen Brittain

Library of Congress Cataloging-in-Publication Data
Names: Glass, Calliope author | Borio, Laura illustrator
Title: Clap, stomp, sing: tales of extraordinary women / by Calliope Glass; illustrated by Laura Borio.
Description: Mankato: Black Rabbit Books, 2026. | Series: Little rebels | Audience: Ages 3–6 | Audience: Grades K–1
Identifiers: LCCN 2025021366 | ISBN 9781645825739 library binding
Subjects: LCSH: Women musicians—Juvenile literature | LCGFT: Picture books
Classification: LCC ML82 G59 2026 | DDC 780.92/52—dc23/eng/20250502
LC record available at https://lccn.loc.gov/2025021366

Printed in China

Clap, Stomp, and Sing

Tales of Extraordinary Women

Text by Calliope Glass | Illustrations by Laura Borio

LOVE ROCK
Strum, strum, strum
the strings

like Joan!

Bang,
tap,
and beat
the drums

like Nandi!

Shimmy, shimmy, shake your hips

like
Carmen!

clap,
clap,
clap
your hands

like
Celia!

and spin
Leap, twirl,

like Misty!

Strut,
smile,
and
strike
a pose

like
Iman!

Wave,
point,
and lead

like Xian!

RESPECT
LOVE
March, chant, sing, and
change the world

PEACE
like Buffy!

Stomp your feet!
Clap your hands!

Raise your voice!
You will make the world a more beautiful place.

JOAN JETT

Singer, songwriter, guitarist, and music producer Joan Jett was born on September 22, 1958, in Pennsylvania. Joan fell in love with music as a child and was given her first guitar when she was 13 years old. She went on to form two bands, the Runaways and Joan Jett and the Blackhearts. Her hit songs like "Cherry Bomb" and "I Love Rock 'n' Roll" still get crowds rocking out today.

NANDI BUSHELL

At 13 years old, Nandi Bushell has played on some of the biggest stages in music. Born in South Africa in 2010, Nandi and her family moved to England when she was two years old. As a reward for her good grades, Nandi's parents got her a drum set. With her dad's help, Nandi shared her covers of popular songs on social media. Her videos went viral! Now, Nandi performs with famous musicians all over the world.

CARMEN MIRANDA

With a colorful look all her own, Carmen Miranda was a popular singer, dancer, and actor. Born in Portugal in 1909, Carmen was raised in Brazil. From a young age, she dreamed of a career in show business. After her first hit record in 1930, she became a star in Brazil. Carmen sang and danced in movie musicals and on Broadway before heading to Hollywood, where she made more than a dozen films.

CELIA CRUZ

Singer Celia Cruz was born on October 21, 1925, in Havana, Cuba. She always loved salsa music. Celia performed with a popular band in Cuba before a revolution broke out and she was forced to leave the country. In the United States, Celia recorded more than 80 albums and became known as the Queen of Salsa. Her energetic performances and distinctive voice made her a beloved figure in music.

MISTY COPELAND

Born on September 10, 1982, Misty Copeland is an American ballet dancer. In 2015, Misty made history as the first Black woman to be promoted to principal dancer in the world-famous dance company, the American Ballet Theatre. Misty discovered dance when she was 13 years old and never looked back. Her grace, strength, and determination have broken barriers and inspired countless young dancers to pursue their dreams.

IMAN

Supermodel and businesswoman Iman was born in Somalia in 1955. When war broke out, she and her family immigrated to Kenya. When she was approached by a well-known photographer in Nairobi, Kenya, her modeling career took off. Iman moved to New York City and appeared on runways, in magazines, and in movies all over the world. Later, she launched a successful makeup brand designed for women of color. Today, Iman uses her influence to do philanthropic work.

XIAN ZHANG

Orchestra conductor Xian Zhang was born in China in 1973 and learned to play music on a piano her dad built for her! Xian started studying conducting at 16 years old and made her first conducting appearance at 19 with the China National Opera Orchestra. Xian went on to conduct prestigious orchestras around the world. She is currently the musical director of the New Jersey Symphony.

BUFFY SAINTE-MARIE

Born on February 20, 1941, Buffy Sainte-Marie is a Native Canadian singer-songwriter, musician, and social activist. Buffy was born on Piapot 75 Reserve in Canada but was sadly taken from her family when she was a toddler. Buffy was raised by adoptive parents in America, but she never forgot her Native roots. Her music explores themes of Indigenous rights, war, and love, touching the hearts of many.

LOVE
ROCK